A Poet's

Cigar Journal
and Ten Poems

Chris Khatsch

To my father and grandfathers

Foreword

Imagine reading the diaries of a poet.

This poet is in his thirties.
He's a simple man who works hard and loves hard.
But he also knows how to party like a hedonist.

You are reading his book now.
You are in his book.

In here,
every line is a breath,
every stanza is a pickled moment,
and every entry is a train of thought
adorned with the poet's emotions
and spirit.

What you'll be reading are not only poems.
They are descriptions of time on fire.

The works in this book are the poetic journal entries
of the poet in his thirties
who smokes and drinks
and works, and works, and works,
then writes
a few words whenever he finds the time to do so.

As you will very soon find out,
this poet is obsessed with cigars
and their philosophical signification.
The aroma of burning tobacco leaves helps him
process the world around him.
Something wakes up in him every time he lights up

a cigar.
He even believes that smoking cigars makes us
more human.
He simply can't stop talking about cigars.
But that's not all he talks about,
as you'll shortly see.

You have picked up a pickle jar filled with
observations,
a photo album filled with pictures of smoke and fire,
and it's time for you to reexperience
what was once experienced by the poet.

But before you begin, it is worth mentioning that
most of the works in this book were already
published or performed elsewhere.
For instance,
the poem called "Once on a Sandy Beach in Tyre"
was published on Eunoia Review in April 2020.
"A Pint of Blood" was performed in many pubs and
bars throughout the years and was published
on multiple websites.
Most of the cigar journal entries were posted
on the poet's blog between 2021 and 2022.
And so on, and so on…

But don't worry! You are not too late, and you won't
be disappointed.
The poet put this book together for you,
dear reader.
He is certain you will say, "I'm glad I read this book.
How could I have not heard of it before! I need a
cigar!"

And now, as you enter the domain of the poet, he promises you this:

The words in this book are of the highest quality.
They were produced in the mind of a pleasure
seeker
who read the best books,
smoked the best cigars,
and drank the best whiskies
he could find.

For the best experience, you are advised to read
this book
in a cigar lounge.

Enjoy,
but remember that smoking is bad for you.

Chris Khatsch
November 24, 2022

A Poet's Cigar Journal

The Man Enters His Cave

A bearded man with an aquiline nose,
with blue eyes turned grey from the cold,
sinks in a leather armchair after a long day,
exhales the world slowly,
and inhales solitude.

At last! he finds himself in a lounge
where thoughts don't leak from mouths,
where ideas don't turn to noise.

He calls the waiter and says,
"Please bring me an Islay whisky.
I would like to taste earth and fire."

As he waits for his drink,
our hero – the bearded man
with the aquiline nose –
pulls out a cigar
from the inside pocket of his jacket
and smells it.
He cuts it, licks it, lights it,
and leans back in the leather armchair.

The whisky comes.
The smoke rises.

The man enters his cave.

King on a Hill

In a folding picnic armchair
our man sat like a king on a hill
after a decisive battle.

The orange moon smiled before it was shrouded by
the smoke
that crept upward
like a dead man's soul.

A cheap cigar danced to the rhythm of classic rock
songs
like a magician's wand (burning)
like a conductor's baton (on fire)
communicating musical ideas
celebrating life
despite the turmoil, tumult, and turbulence.

The cigar was a paint brush
and the night sky was an empty canvas.
Gray on black: a seductive belly dance.
Gray on black: the last breath of a soldier.

Our man felt a poem being written
somewhere,
a poem written phenomenologically
now.

"Yes, yes," our man said right now.
"So the muses came like they often do
when they smell a cigar burn."

And then he jotted down whatever came to him.

As I Waited for My Fiancée to Get Dressed

Waiting on the balcony of a five-star hotel room,
I remembered Roland Barthes's words,
"Am I in love? - Yes, since I'm waiting."

I looked at my watch;
it told me I had time.
So, I waited.
I waited a long time.

A cool breeze caressed me sporadically as dusk
fell slowly.

I could hear the tick and tock of an invisible clock
that made me want to think and talk
(do anything, in fact)
to repel boredom, delay boredom
as much as I can.

I wanted to say, "Hurry up."
But I didn't. I had to wait.
I knew
because I was in love.

And so, I waited
until I saw the silhouette of Boredom
ambling toward me.
What a sight!
It disturbed me deeply.
I did not want to see its face!

It is Death with a human mask – Boredom is!

It is the state of being unoccupied in a busy world,
the state of being left out,
the state of not having a thing to do.

It is the Reaper's old wristwatch.

I had to act quickly!
So, I decided to start to celebrate immediately!
Even if it meant celebrating
without
the company of the one I love.

I went in to bring
a book, a drink, and a cigar –
my three musketeers.

My fiancée, who was putting on makeup,
asked, "What are you doing?"
I replied, "Waiting."

I stepped outside again
bravely – back on the balcony
where the cool breeze caressed me sporadically
as dusk fell slowly.
This time, I was carrying the tools
that would help me ward off boredom.

And as I waited for my fiancée to get dressed for
her birthday party,
I nursed my drink and smoked my cigar.

I realized I was no longer waiting,
although I was still in love.

I was celebrating (reading) (drinking) (smoking),
celebrating

like a hard-working man should
after a long day
or after a long week.

Something was happening.

In the book I was reading, Rousseau was saying,
"We covet knowledge merely because we covet
enjoyment."

I was underlining sentences I found interesting,
nodding, agreeing,
keeping myself busy…

I was no longer waiting.
I was no longer waiting.

My First Cuban

I inhaled the night.
I inhaled the night like I used to in Hamra
but this time in Broummana.

The year: 2021.
The month: July.
Temperature: Hot.
Humidity: High.

Bars and restaurants were swarming with
hungry, horny, thirsty
people (hedonistic automatons)
as usual
as if Covid-19 was already history,
as if the Lebanese pound was strong and stable,
as if the Beirut port explosion never happened,
blah, blah, (I'm so drunk writing this)
and all the brouhaha.

Cars honked at high heels and tight dresses.
The valets then took those cars and parked them in
parallel universes.

I inhaled the night.

I could smell the perfumes of rivals in a love
triangle.
I could smell the sweat of the working class, the
hard workers.
I could smell garbage and sulfur.

The ghosts of
the dreams and desires of my generation
filled my lungs.

I needed to burn something.
I needed a smoke.

The hostess took me to the table
where my friends were sitting,
chit-chatting, already moving
to the beat.

That night,
I tasted what Lebanon could have been,
and I tasted my first Cuban cigar.

"For never was a story of more woe than this of
Juliet and her Romeo."

As the electronic beats' vibrations massaged my
glutes,
I smoked, and
I observed the night.

I saw Beauty in a long-term relationship with
Sadness.
I saw Past and Present sitting on high stools facing
one another,
smoking cigarettes and sharing memories.
There was a third stool at their table, but it was
empty.

I drank. I observed.
I ordered many drinks, and I drank
while I observed.

Yes, well, it seemed everyone was outdoors
living in a bubble of loud and bassy music
as if they weren't suffering, or mourning, or dying.

There was life.
But where the music did not reach, life did not
either.

Hedonists everywhere! And I was a hedonist
partying like
après moi, le déluge.
Every now and then, one must party like
après moi, le déluge.

So, I drank until everybody was drunk.

But though we were partying like free spirits,
I knew we weren't free at all.
We were, in fact, afraid of freedom.
We were, in fact, only acting like we were free.

Paulo Freire said it right in Pedagogy of the
Oppressed.
"Freedom is acquired by conquest, not by gift.
It must be pursued constantly and responsibly."

"Drink Responsibly," the sign said.
(I'm so drunk writing this.)

And "It is solely by risking life that freedom is
obtained," Hegel said
in one of his books.
But we are not ready to risk anything.
We lost everything.
We don't have the means to risk anything.

Let me tell you,
the air was so humid all foreheads shined like stars.

Drunken Sisyphus

I woke up with a hangover,
ready to work on another hangover.
I am like a Sisyphus whose bottle refills
every time it is emptied.

This is my life, then.
This is where I am now.
Madness cannot be very far from here.
You can see that in my sunken eyes —
how exhausted I am!
And burned out. And bored out.

In between hangovers, there is some
suffering
and a lot of drinking.
In between hangovers, there is the life
that I never wanted… except
the love story that's being written.

I smoke cigars, too, when I drink.
Often, the cheapest cigars I can find;
other times,
cigars that burn like Shakespeare's plays in a
fireplace.

And you can smell the fire in my beard
and all the verses I have burned
under the open sky.

When I drink, I like to have a pen
and a notebook in proximity, too.
But I see how this may mislead the onlooker.

You must never mistake me for a poet
even if you see me scribble
and spit out words like active volcanoes spit out
lava.

Where I come from, poems give birth to
themselves.
The poet is the drunkard who happens to be there
when it happens.

Where I come from, the poet has not mastered the
language.
On the contrary, he has given up on language;
he merely uses it out of boredom,
distorts it, abuses it…

Where I come from, the poem is only read by the
poet
who will forget
everything.

In the morning, nothing will exist but a hangover
that means nothing at all.

Celebrate

When you can celebrate,
celebrate.

What can I say?

This life is for rent.
It will be over
sooner than you'd like.
So don't waste it on stupid things,
and don't work too hard.
You cannot buy eternity
no matter how rich you are.

I'm not sure what it cost us
to be born.
But we must have paid a high price
to rent our lives.
So make the best of it.
Time isn't cheap. And
if you can celebrate,
celebrate.

What more can I say?

When your time is up, it is up.
You just drop.
You won't get that five more minutes to say
I love you or goodbye.

That's what I learned from dad.
I was at work when I got the call.
It was already

game over. Adios.
Bye-bye, daddio.

What can I say?

I miss the man.
We could have had more beers together.
We could have talked more,
hugged more,
celebrated more.

But he's gone now.
So, game over. Adios.

You never get to say goodbye.

Never mind.
Never mind.

When you can celebrate,
celebrate.
Don't wait for occasions.
Don't try to make things perfect,
it's a waste of time.

A good smoke, a good drink,
and a few good memories
are all you need.

Yeah, I have many good memories,
and tonight, I celebrate with them.

Cheers, dad.

Echoes of a Blast

Here I am smoking an excellent Cuban cigar on a balcony overlooking Beirut and the Mediterranean Sea. It is 11:15 AM on a weekday in September. The sky is clear, and my panoramic view tinted by the rays of a cheerful sun does not lack splendor or beauty.

I can see the Beirut port from here, the same one that exploded last year. And I can see large cargo ships patiently waiting to deliver the goods they carry. The sea looks calm and serene.

Briefly, I let my eyes focus on the narrow line that separates the land from the sea. I see tiny cars on the highway flowing towards Beirut. Like blood cells, the cars go in and out of Beirut. "The heart still beats," I say to myself. "This broken heart, despite everything, still beats."

Everything looks alright in this picture. From a distance, everything looks just fine. But I know that what I'm looking at is, in fact, a place that can only be described as hell. I cannot see the suffering from here, yet I know it's there.

I smoke my cigar and take notes in my notebook.

When I am done smoking, my eyes let go of Beirut and the sea, and I go inside to make coffee.

I Turn My Back on The Sun

I turn my back on the sun and light a cigar.
The sunset and the sea mean nothing to me.

I am overwhelmed with thoughts.
There's always so much work to do,
always so much work left
for me to do.

It's like my mind can never leave
the workplace.
My mind can never punch out.

I'm on standby all the time,
forever ready to receive an email
outside working hours.

No matter how efficient I am,
I will never accomplish enough
to deserve a good break.

I draw and blow white smoke
as businesses live and die.

Ghosts of CEOs and COOs slither out of my mouth,
and they all look like the man
in Edvard Munch's The Scream.
They all look the same to me.

I want to scream, too,
but the neighbors may think I'm crazy.
So,
I turn my back on the sun and light a cigar.

You, the Wife, and the Dog

There's you,
your wife,
and the dog.

The dog's licking rocks,
chewing on branches,
and eating grass.

The wife is sitting on a picnic blanket,
sipping on vodka
while tanning her shoulders.

You're looking at her,
asking yourself, "How
can I make her the happiest person
on earth?"

You're an average man
coming from a working-class family.
Boy, just a few years ago,
you couldn't afford a good steak.
Surprise, surprise, yo.
You didn't see yourself
living the life,
did you?
The nice apartment,
the hot wife,
and everything else that you love so much right
now.
You thought, "Nah,
it's never going to happen 'cause I'm poor."

But you forget
your father raised a hard-working man.
Your mother put fire in your soul.

Man…
What a ride!
Have a sip of beer.

You were a nobody,
and you're still a nobody,
a nobody who
likes to read, write, drink,
and smoke cigars.
Yeah, nobody knows you,
but aren't you exactly who you want to be
right now? Aren't you
who you weren't meant to be?

Wake up, son!
You had a lot to drink.
But that was a good nap.

There's sun in your eyes,
sweat on your brow,
mustard on your shirt.

But it's alright if you smile.
Smile, you son of a gun!
Yeah,
when you add it all up,
you're happy.

How did you manage to be so happy?

Wake up, son!
It's time to play with the dog.
It's time to kiss your wife.

It's time to know you're happy.

Cigar on a Sunny Day

I smoked a cigar on a sunny day.
It was my first cigar of the day.

It was a small gift
from a close friend.

I smoked it in the woods,
in the afternoon,
in my hiking boots.

I smoked it on a very good day,
in good company.

We grilled meat
in an atmosphere filled with –
manliness.

So, I cannot help but love this cigar.

Three Drinks with Every Cigar

Cigar lounges in Lebanon normally close at 10:00 PM,
which is sad.

But my friends and I measure time
with cigars, not watches.

When I'm with out with the boys
putting some smoke in the air,
reaching the final third of the cigar
means that
we don't have much time left.
It's like a pub's last call, if you like.

Coincidentally, when I reach the final third
of my cigar, I usually order my last drink.

On average, I have three drinks with every cigar
I smoke.

Today, I had two cigars.
That means I had six drinks.

There are really two paths a man can take.

The first path is pairing the cigar with the drink.
The second path is pairing the drink with the cigar.

When I'm at a cigar lounge, I do the latter.
This means that I choose the cigar first,
and I order my drink only after I light my cigar.
Sometimes, when the pairing is successful,
I stick with the same drink.

I have three of the same.
If I'm having peated whisky, for example,
I'll have three glasses of the same whisky.
If I'm having rum, I'll have two more glasses
of the same rum.

Other times, when the pairing is unsuccessful,
or when the aficionado in me demands it,
I have three different drinks,
pairing one with every third
of the cigar.

When I'm at a gathering or a party, however,
I am forced to pair the cigar with the drink.
That means I'll have to choose a cigar that goes
well with the beverage that's being offered.
So, I choose my cigar based on what's available.
And that's not a problem
because I always carry more than one cigar with
me.

One must carry more than one cigar with him
at all times,
so that one never feels like
he's out of options
or
he doesn't have much time left.

Reading Fear and Trembling

Reading Fear and Trembling,
daydreaming,
smoking a cigar like I control time,
staring into Abraham's eyes,
smelling morning in the afternoon,
drinking black coffee.
I feel the wind caress my face.
I'm thinking,
assimilating.
"The one who works will give
birth to his own father."

I'm looking for Camus, Kafka,
Beckett, and their friends.
I'm thinking about Erich Fromm's
and Ernest Becker's
texts.

No one understands,
and no one will understand
why I read, I live, I write.

I want to explain,
but I don't want to waste my time.

Bourj Hammoud

On a terrace somewhere in Bourj Hammoud
the waiter leaves our table with empty bottles
and comes back with new drinks

He seems to be trapped in a never-ending loop

We drink

We talk politics
disagree
then talk about Paris

I light a second cigar

We head to another bar

Barbecue

I wake up tired, dreams leaking, mouth dry.
I kiss my wife, "Good morning, love."
Then I jump out of bed like a cat out of a trash can
and go downstairs to make coffee.

Another day. More work. Isn't that my life?
But it's Friday, so I work half day.
Look! It's a sunny day.
Can't let this go to waste.

"Me, you, and barbecue," I tell my wife.
"How romantic of you," she says as she smiles.
"I'm serious," I say.
"Let's do it," she says.

Fire,
meat,
a bottle of premium Scotch whisky,
and a good cigar.

The sun is shining like there are no misfortunes in
the world,
like work isn't stressful and anxiety attacks are
unheard of,
like death doesn't exist,
like life is devoid of suffering,
like Lucifer is still God's favorite angel.

The sun is shining,
and my loved one is sitting next to me.
Maybe I can call myself happy.
Right now. Happy.

Blurring Reality with Smoke

I could smell
the leather armchair of a philosopher
misplaced and forgotten in a chocolate factory.

I could taste
the sweetened pain of a man biting on a leather belt
in a torture chamber.

Where does the sadism come from?

I could taste earth, wood, and chickpeas
dissolved in coffee —
muddy, Arabic coffee.

I was smoking a cigar
and nursing a twelve-year-old whisky.

"This is a good cigar," I said to my wife
who was busy witnessing the synthesis of
people, music, and alcohol
in a failed state.

The music was loud,
the lights were dim,
the people were
cocktail-drinking, popcorn-eating zombies
wasting their lives.

Were they trapped in this city
and the best they could do was
party?

Was I not like them? There,
burning valuable time.
Waiting, maybe, for something.

I was there smoking
time
like I could smoke eternity
without ever feeling bored.

I was there blurring reality
with smoke.

A Short Break

Finally, after a long day, a short break.

I need an earthquake
to shake me out of work
this evening.

What a day.

I'm glad I managed to escape
the world
to come here and hide
on the roof of a six-story building.

All I want to do is burn a cigar,
watch the smoke rise,
and listen to the fire crawl.

I've got nothing to say
other than I've got nowhere to be,
no one to see.

I'm here alone
to be alone.

Finally, after a long day, a short break.

The Genius and the Introvert

The genius isn't the madman.
The genius
is the one who realizes that
to be mad is the only reasonable thing to do.
Therefore,
he lives madly.

And I want to live madly so badly,
but the world doesn't let me,
and I'm so cowardly.

As for the introvert, – beware! –
this one isn't an introvert.
He is an observer, a thinker, a plotter,
who doesn't want you to see what's in his eyes.

I know because I smoke cigars with him
when I'm alone.

Walking the Dog

You're a little drunk.
You decide to take the dog for a walk
and smoke a cigar while you're at it.
But the dog ends up walking you instead.
You realize that when you find yourself
pissing under a tree
while the dog is sitting next to you
waiting for you to finish.

Keep it Burning

A full-bodied cigar,
dark
with notes of fearlessness and passion.

It burns majestically, cheerfully,
nostalgically like memories
shared
when you're at a bar
with one of the best friends
life could give you.

Beer mugs are emptied
one after another.
Laughter…

Shots of whiskey are downed
like rounds of bullets,
with every shot killing a bad joke,
a bad day,
a bad memory.

Stories are told…

Drunkenness wraps itself
around your heart and your tongue.

Yes.

Sometimes,
you enjoy the moment so much
that you forget about space and time.
Sometimes,
you enjoy the cigar so much

that you forget something is burning
in your hand.

But you know this,
that always
fire is leisure,
love and life.
It is everything but
darkness and forgetfulness.

So, you keep it burning
this fire that you have —
the cigar, the grill, the fireplace…
And never put it out
because, when you do,
tediousness will swallow you
and you will want to die.

Smoking on the Balcony

Cold, windy night.
Winding down on the balcony
in a trench coat.
Listening to the rain
that sounds like fire
devouring crunchy stone pine branches.

I comb my thick beard with my fingers.
I feel the cold resting on my face.
I try to brush it off — the cold —
unsuccessfully.

Yesterday was a good day.
Today is a good day, too.
There's work, yes, but also time to rest.

It's freezing, though.
My fingers want to snuggle into my pockets
and cuddle with the cutter and the lighter.
But they have work to do.

In thirty minutes,
when I'm done drinking and smoking,
I'll go inside and sit by the fireplace.
I'll give my fingers their well-deserved rest.
Maybe I'll turn on the TV and have a cup of tea.

Not All Cigars Are Burning Poems

Words preserved in pages
like torshi seer in mason jars
don't mean
what they used to mean.
But they are much more meaningful now.

Not all cigars are burning poems.
Some of them are hourglasses.
Others are daydreams.

Their purpose changes.

Who has a raison d'être? Show me.
Isn't the meaning constantly changing?
Are you here for the same reason
you were here yesterday?
Even if you think so, you're not.
You don't have a purpose,
you have many;
therefore, none at all.

Hangover

The morning came.
The hangover came with it
again
like a great song that has become annoying
because it was forgotten on repeat.

Why do I constantly
"drain the dregs of pleasure's bowl"
when I'm aware that regret
will crow like a rooster at dawn?

Maybe because
the cigars that I smoke
and the whiskies that I drink
intensify my pleasure
and help me summarize
the events of the world
and the sweet and salty moments
of life
in a way that nothing else can.

And maybe not.

Maybe because I can only stand
the absurdity of reality
and the stupidity of people
when I am wasted.

And maybe not.

Nonetheless, the question must be asked aloud.
Is a hangover a good price to pay?
I think it is

if you plan on getting wasted
occasionally – when you must.

Windy Day

The wind is blowing hard,
screaming in my ears,
pushing away the grey clouds,
making room for spring.

I go in and come back out
with a new cigar, a cutter,
and a triple jet torch lighter
to celebrate the new sun,
although I know well
that wind is the enemy
of cigars.

I give my cigar a straight cut
and wait
for the right time to
toast it
and light it.

The wind stops blowing.
"You have only a moment to light your cigar."
"Thank you."

As soon as I take my first draw,
the wind continues to scream
mercilessly
until my cigar starts to burn unevenly,
until I can no longer hear the world

Petrichor

This cigar tastes like petrichor
and the cool afternoon shade of a tall tree by the
river
mixed with the sweat of a hard-working man
accompanied by the aroma of hand-picked coffee
beans
and cedar
and hints of pink peppercorn.

It tastes like the last storm of March
and the mud of early April.

Overloaded

Overloaded. Overbooked. Overtired.

I'm becoming busier and busier with things that
don't matter a lot to me.

But they're necessary.

Heavy work.
Responsibilities.
Side hustles.

I can't escape the constriction coil
of the corporate snake.

Where is my freedom?

I'm just happy that I'm still finding time to smoke an
occasional cigar.

When You Start Pairing Cigars with Wines

When you start pairing cigars with wines,
remind yourself that you're in a very good place.

Be proud.
You've come a long way, and it's your hard work
and discipline
that got you here.
You owe nothing to nobody.

Bravo.

Don't postpone the celebration.
You are in good health,
surrounded by loved ones,
and the sun is shining like there will never
be a cloudy day again.

Don't wait.
Come on!
Celebrate.

Smoke a good cigar.
Drink a little more than usual.
Laugh a little louder.

Own it.

I Used to Wait for a Good Occasion

I used to wait for a good occasion
to light a cigar.
When I think about it now,
I shake my head and smile.

Why do I need to wait
for someone to get married
for me to light up a stick?
Why does it have to be an engagement,
or a bachelor, or a baptism,
or a birthday party
or anything?

These days, I don't care.
I just want to feel good.
I burn six to seven a week.
I smoke everywhere,
everywhere I can.

I'd light one up at a funeral, too,
if I had the chance.
I don't mind.
It's not only on happy occasions that a man
needs a smoke.

Working-Class Man's Cigar

I'm smoking a working-class man's cigar
on the terrace,
drinking,
thinking about the past
and the masks I had to wear
to get here,
to a place so near
to the stars…

I'm thinking about my father
and how he would have enjoyed smoking cigars
and drinking beer
with me.
He would have been proud…

I believe I'm where I want to be,
but there are other places I need to be.
There are all sorts of hats I need to wear,
all sorts of shoes I need to fill,
and so on,
and so forth.
And there are dreams I need to kill,
all sorts of destinies I need to fulfill,
and so on,
and so on forever, it seems.

Smoking a cigar on the terrace,
I'm texting a friend
whose cigar didn't burn as well as mine
today.
And doesn't this remind me of
something incomprehensible called

luck,
and how lucky I am to possess it?

I'm getting hints of earth.
I'm thinking, "I'll get a lot of it
when they finally bury me."
I'm getting hints of maple and honey.
This is how sweet life tastes right now.

What a night to be alive!
I will refill my glass now.
And when I come back out, I will shout,
"What a night to be alive!"

I will refill my glass now,
and I will do so until
I have no more dreams to kill
and no memories to remember.
I will refill my glass and sing
until it's time for me to sleep.

A Wonderful Place

A wonderful place.

A place where philosophy is paired
with fat cigars,
full-bodied, aromatic cigars
that produce a lot of smoke,
creamy, thick, slithering smoke.

Poetry, here, is not read;
it is drunk from tumblers and highballs.
And time is measured by drams and draws
and vitolas.

Sometimes, I come here to forget
work-related stress.
Other times, I come here for a game of chess.
But most of the times, I'm here simply
for the slow-burning cigars and fireside chats.

To sink in these leather armchairs
is to enter a world of —
How can I put it?
I'll have to think about it.
But not now. Later.
Now, it's time to enter the humidor
again
and pick a cigar that will take me there
again

Brother of the Leaf

My friend and I exit the humidor,
each of us holding two cigars.
I intend to smoke both tonight,
and I'm sure he intends to do the same.

Let me be more precise.
This friend of mine
is my brother
of the leaf.

Cigar lounges are where we meet
and talk.
Our conversations take us everywhere
— we travel the world and the mind
sitting in leather armchairs.

We talk about cigars:
"Look at the abundant smoke coming out of this
cigar."
We talk about women:
"She's stunning. But she's still young and innocent."
We talk about balls.
"He had the balls to do it. But you have to be a little
stupid to have so much balls."
Yes, we talk about everything
— the focus is always
being a man.

When we light our cigars,
we exit the world

and look at it
from above,
from below,
and from the sides.

And when you join us,
we will say,
"Welcome to the cave. Have a cigar."

You Can't Always Get What You Want

There will be good days, and there will be bad
days.
Sometimes, you'll experience success; other times,
you'll encounter failure.
And it's not always about you
or how good you are.

My friend who is a big-time cigar smoker knows
this.
He says that even the best cigar brands disappoint
you occasionally.
The one who rolled it may be to blame,
or the one who stored it,
or the one who smoked it.
The place and the people you're with also matter.
They matter a lot.

So, when you have a bad day,
accept it.
Don't lose it, brother.
Keep it cool.
Find a cave.

As it is wearily sung in the chorus of one of the best
songs
of The Rolling Stones, "You can't
always get what you want."
No, you can't always get what you want.
And whether you're a stoic or not, you'll have to
accept that
sooner or later.

You have the power to make things happen,
to change something in the world,
to change the whole world.

However, when you're out there trying hard,
remember that
while you try to make things happen,
things will happen to you, too.
Before you change the world,
the world might change you.

Don't be afraid.

Debauchery

I believe I will pass out in a minute or two,
but, before that, I must confess a thing or two.

I have a big tendency to be a hedonist.
I was born to be one. Actually,
I am one,
and everyone knows it, including
my mother, my sister, and my wife.

Debauchery has always been a recurring word in
my vocabulary.
I often send the word alone as a message
with only a question mark next to it.
And when my friend — or to be more exact, my
accomplice — receives it,
all he has to do is answer with a yes or a no.
"Debauchery?"
"Yes. I sure do hope so."

If you know me, you know
I get carried away easily.
When it's a song I love, I sing along.
And one beer can easily turn to five, or six, or
twelve.
Same goes for whisky shots.

"Have a drink on me, poet!"

The world is spinning,
and I feel like I'm the center of the universe.

Let me tell you about the smell of the night:
the beer, the whisky, the smoke,
and the perfumes worn by all these women
I cannot touch —
although, I do occasionally get a napkin
with a drawing of a heart, a phone number,
and a name on it.
But I leave them all on the bar top,
so that they know I'm not interested,
even though I am sometimes tempted.
I enjoy the smell of sweat and skin.
But when I howl, I howl at the moon, not them.

My impulses are my masters,
but I don't follow them blindly.
I may follow the footsteps of drunkards,
but I'm always tightrope walking.
Never a wrong step, except maybe
the excessive drinking.
But that's because I get carried away too easily.
Yes, I get carried away too easily.
I know, and I'm afraid.
I'm afraid
because I know what I'm capable of doing.
I have the power to ruin my life,
to destroy everything I have built so far
in an instant.

I go in and out of bars, in and out of bars,
and my fire is always burning —
there's always a cigarette or a cigar
burning.

What am I really chasing?
Celebration.

What am I celebrating?
I don't know.
It's the feeling of drowning that I love…
You'll never understand!

My life may not have any meaning,
but that doesn't make me stop
dreaming.
That doesn't make me stop
wanting.

The smoke is always dancing.
The smoke is always dancing.

Cocaine of the Masses

On a balcony overlooking the Port of Beirut,
you and your friend are smoking
one of the best cigars you smoked so far this year.

You're talking politics
to pass the time.
Sunday, everyone is voting it seems,
except you.
Marx was right when he said, "Religion
is the opium of the people."
But he forgot to add,
"Politics is the cocaine of the masses."
Can one really be apolitical, though?
No.
You say you'll think about this tomorrow,
whether you'll vote or not,
but you know you won't.
You are incapable of
giving a shit.

"It is what it is," you start concluding.
You look at your friend and say,
"Let's have another glass, and then
you can drive me home."

Time slows down
to let you paint the black night grey.
Smoke rises to kiss the moon.
The cigar burns like a dying star.

Old Friend

The doorbell rings.
You let the old friend in.

"Come in, come in!
Where have you been?
Come in, old friend,
and have a cigar."

He comes with a gift
— a bottle of Scotch.
"Thank you!
You didn't have to!
I'll open it now!"

You bring him the humidor.
"Here," you say,
"Choose one that you love."
"You have good taste," he says,
"Please, choose one for me."

You light one up,
and he lights one up.
You pour the Scotch,
and then you pour some rum.

Politics,
philosophy,
work,
and women.

You drink, you smoke, you talk,
you talk,
and then he says,
"It's late. I must leave."

Ten Poems

A Pint of Blood

"Poetry is the devil's inbox."

But daytime was no time to philosophize.
So we hung about cheap coffee shops
Sipped espressos on dirty sidewalks.

We, five poets with empty wallets,
The modern prophets,
Lived our lives in between big brackets,
Smoked cigarettes,
Wasted sunsets,
Et cetera, et cetera…

Now Time
For the sun to sink into the silver sea
And die.

Time
For the son of sin to feel her skin
For the snake to slither between her thighs
And why
Not post it on Facebook
Or be a Twitter god?

And Time
For us, the poets with bad habits,
To invade the pubs and bars of Hamra Street
Looking here and there if someone's rolling
Weed, hashish, or Red Lebanese…

But nighttime was no time to philosophize either.
So we hung about cheap bars and pubs
Drinking beer on dirty sidewalks.

And then the girls with no names came,
Their laughter: sex notes
And R&B
Champagne and pain
And misery

"I think that one's from X.Y.Z.
I did her at the dorms in November.
She needed money
to pay for her courses."

"You bastard! That's my sister."
A non-poet cried right then
and broke that poet's nose.

Blood in the beer
A pint of blood!
A toast for our brave, bare sister.
Knives and chairs and broken beer bottles…
A fight
A war
A massacre
In which I did not take part.

And all this time, I was thinking,
Eyes wide open, without blinking,
About how a fellow poet
Could pay so much to fuck
When I was paying for his beer.

It's Poetry When

It's poetry when you read it
more than once
and your coffee gets cold.

It's poetry when no one knows it is
but you read it aloud anyway
because of how it sounds.

It's poetry when the greatest poet
says it's not
but you write it down anyway
and he tries to stop you
so you run with it
like a chicken with a pen
up its butt.

The Protester

How many roadblocks on my way to you?

How many streets filled with fists?

Love is strong but not as strong as
U.S. sanctions and currency exchange rates,
power cuts and blackouts,
hunger,
and the ongoing garbage crisis.

Burning tires.

I see black smoke rising.

I put on a facemask and cross the street.
I remove the facemask.
Why are we afraid of death?

Unshaven and exhausted
with a dirty Lebanese flag on my shoulders
and an unlit cigarette drooping from my lips,
I reach Martyrs' Square.

But there is no hope, is there?

Where can we go to keep our love alive?

A Stroll in Geitawi

Whatever isn't supposed to happen
happens
here.

Darkness is heavy.
Darkness is so heavy.

My footsteps are louder than the night.
My future is as dark as
tonight.

The moon keeps hiding behind
thick clouds. It isn't
romantic.
It's just the silver eye of a cowardly god
peeping in.

Beirut can't afford a good night.
Beirut can't afford light.

My footsteps are louder than the night.
I can't hear
my brothers and sisters crying.

I Cannot Log in to Reality

I can't stay
away from screens.

I barely exist
in the physical world.

For maintenance only.

I disconnect to eat or to defecate.
I reconnect for work and leisure,
like I was meant to become data.

And like a fly tangled in a spider web,
it seems, I cannot escape
the World Wide Web.

The ghost of my existence clings
to the Internet of Things,
where the virtualized forms
of everyone and everything
dwell.

And things don't happen anymore.
They don't take place in the physical world.
And when they do, they echo in the metaverse.
I don't exist anymore –
at least, not in the world I used to know.

Is this the beginning of
the technological singularity prophesied,

or are we already worshipping
the all-seeing tarantula?

We're all chained to blockchains now.

When I turn off my devices,
who do I become?
And how do I get rid of this brain fog?

I cannot log in to Reality.
I'm there for maintenance only –
to charge batteries and
take care of basic physiological needs.

I cannot really log in to Reality.

Forgot password.

I must go back.

I must turn on
smartphone, computer, tablet, smartwatch
now.

Authenticating… Connecting…

must
surf.

must
serf.

Connected.

Good morning, Nightmare

Good morning, nightmare.
Work begins in 30 minutes.

I'm in my flip-flops, standing near the stove, waiting
for the water to boil.
I'm holding a mug that contains grains of instant
coffee and sands of time.
A spoon leans idly in the mug.
When the time comes, it will stir up things.
But not now.

Work
from
home.

Work
starts
now.

Silent mode: off.
A big mistake.
I start receiving notifications.
"I am following up on…"
"I am waiting for the…"
"When will we be able to…"
"Can you please…"
"It's urgent."

I wish I could find a way out
of this dystopia.

Silent mode: on.
A bad idea.
But it will give me five minutes
to be myself.

Untitled

Woke up.
Neck pain. Back pain.
I wore yesterday's clothes.

On my way to work,
the movie "28 Days Later" came to my mind.
Emptiness. Abandoned spaces.
Few cars.
It's the end of the world, I thought.
It's the end of my world.

And now I'm here
smoking a cigarette on the sidewalk,
inhaling the fear of death that's in the air.
This Thursday feels like a Sunday,
but I'm not praying.
I'm thinking: Motherfuckers,
I was looking forward to
open sausages and open beer,
but they just told me
all restaurants are closed until further notice.

Corruption and incompetency.
Impotence.
The economic crisis.
The COVID-19 pandemic.
What's next and what can we do?
We can't run — they're shutting down the airports.
We can't hide — we'll starve.

I can't work.
I can't think.

And now in the office,
in my rolling chair,
I'm trying to get rid of
this brain fog
by scrolling down
my Facebook newsfeed.

Moments ago,
I called the convenience store
and ordered wet wipes and
hand sanitizers.

I'm alone in the office.
There's no one else here.

Time to Become a New Man

Woke up wanting
to become a new man
again.

The birds were singing,
mockingly tweeting
while fragments of pointless conversations
and choruses from the night before
ricocheted in my head.

Memories blown to shreds.
Everything fleeting
except regret.

Thoughts – whirlwinds
in my crumbling mind! –
were like propelled balls
in a pinball machine.

I was crying, "God…
Was I playing
beer pong?
I was. I kept on playing
beer pong,
losing almost every game."

The birds were singing,
"He must become a new,
new man.
The man he is now
is self-destructing."

The Market

Fine shops, cheap shops.
Watch the watches.
Because time,
It passes.
The world is restless.

Outside,
Socrates with a hemlock bottle.
Needs nothing,
Wonders what others need.

Why stop? Must shop!
Sulfur matches.
Because life,
It passes.
You turn to ashes.

Inside,
Well, well, can you smell hell?
Sees nothing,
Wonders what others see.

Once on a Sandy Beach in Tyre

"Got poems on the soles of my shoes,
some lines on my forehead and a stanza full of
clues
in one of my pockets," he whispered in my ear.
We buried him next to his wife. That year
I turned eighteen and grew my first beard.

I came to you because you knew
my grandpa in his teens.
When drunk, he talked about you
—how you peeled tangerines.
He wrote about you, too,
wrote on tiny, torn pieces of paper,
hid them in the holster of the revolver
he sold in the early nineties, after
the end of the civil war.
He kept that worn, brown leather holster
in a worn, brown leather briefcase.
The key to the briefcase he kept in his pocket.

He wrote about the sea, the sweat, the heat,
and your tanned body spread
on a sandy beach in Tyre.
His heart was on fire.
He kissed your lips, tasted sand and salt,
time and tears,
under the sun that melted the ice in the ice bucket.
Then you imbibed rosé from the bottle.
It was now warm, but you drank every drop.
You smiled and asked him if he'd carry you home.

You drew a cedar in the sand;
the waves came and took it.
You drew a heart in the sand;
the waves came and took it.

You held each other until sunset.
You wanted to stay for a little longer.
You would have stayed forever.
But he had run out of cigarettes,
so you had to leave.

You said, "I will buy you beer on our way back."
He said, "I will buy you a rose from that beggar
boy."

On his deathbed, he wrote to you.
That's why I looked for you.
His words are in my pocket,
and this ring belonged to you.

The End

Printed in Great Britain
by Amazon

23665209R00047